1

A ceremony is a used to mark an important event. A wedding is a kind of ceremony. The First Peoples have many important ceremonies.

3

Song and dance are a big part of ceremony for the First Peoples.

5

There are different songs and dances for different ceremonies.

7

Songs and dances would be swapped between groups at large ceremonies.

9

These songs and dances told Dreaming stories. These stories had important lessons for the First Peoples.

11

The didgeridoo might be the world's oldest instrument. Didgeridoos are used in some ceremonies.

13

Dances used in ceremonies are passed down from older people to younger people.

15

There are ceremonies for when a boy becomes a man.

17

Today, dance groups use these old ceremonies to make new shows.

19

Dance is used to show love for family. In some places, dances may be performed at the end of every day.

21

Many ceremonies are sacred.
They are not shown to people
outside the group.

23

Word bank

ceremony

different

family

important

instrument

lessons

older

oldest

performed

sacred

wedding